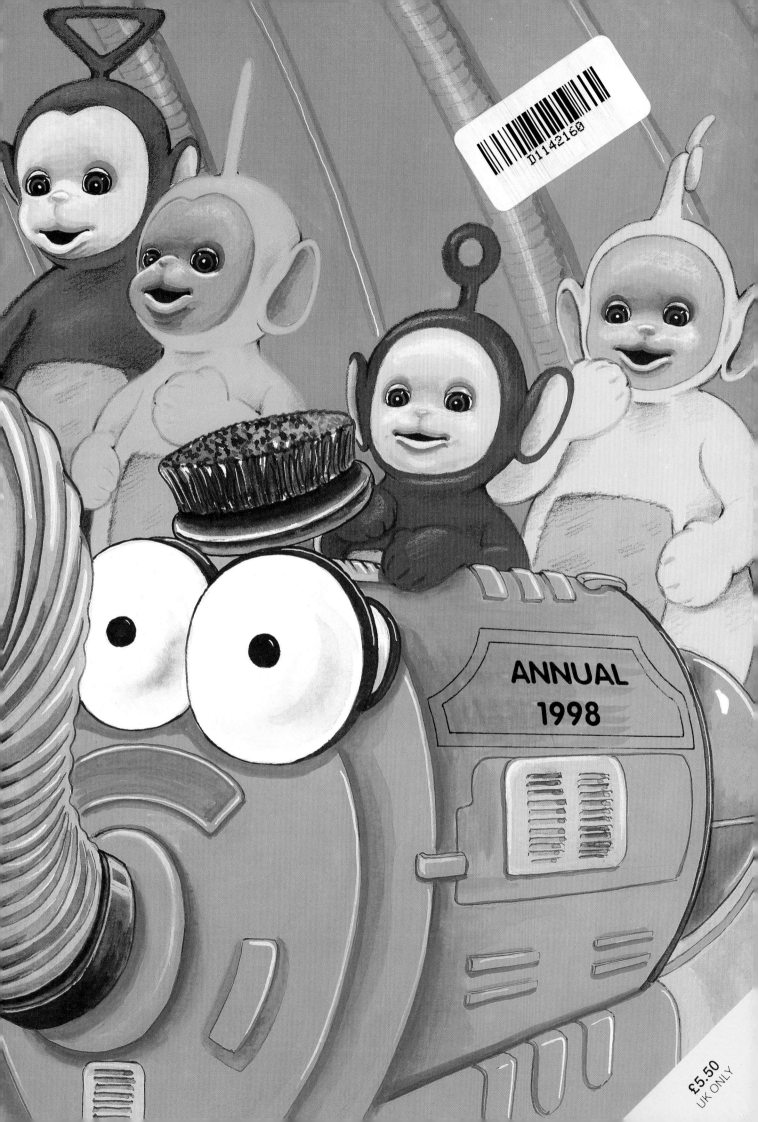

ANNUAL
1998

£5.50
UK ONLY

# This

## Teletubbies™

## 1998 Annual belongs to

..................................

sluuurp! sluuurp!

sluuurp!

Written by Davey Moore, Illustrated by Jane Swift.
Teletubbies characters and logo © &™ 1996 Ragdoll
Productions (UK) Ltd. Licensed by BBC Worldwide Ltd.
CIP data for this book is available from the British Library
Copyright © 1997 World International Ltd.,
Deanway Technology Centre, Wilmslow Road, Handforth,
Cheshire, SK9 3FB. All rights reserved.
Printed in Great Britain. ISBN 0 7498 3385 8

# Contents

5

Over the hills and far away, Teletubbies come to play...
1,2,3,4 Teletubbies

Teletubbies...Teletubbies

Tinky Winky

Dipsy

Laa-Laa

Po

Teletubbies...Teletubbies

Teletubbies say hello!

E-oh!

# Teletubbies...Teletubbies

# Say Hello!

Say hello in all these different languages.

Hello
(hel-LO)
English

Hola
(OH-la)
Spanish

Namaste
(nam-ahs-TAY)
Hindi

Bonjour
(bon-JOR)
French

Guten Tag
(Gu-ten TAHG)
German

Konnichiwa
(kon-E-chi-wa)
Japanese

Buongiorno
(bwon-JOR-noh)
Italian

Hej!
(HEY!)
Swedish

# Our Favourite Things

Teletubbies

Tinky Winky

**Dipsy**

Teletubbies

13

# The Windmill

The Windmill
turns round
and round
and round
and round!

Draw some swirls around
The Windmill and some
more magic stars.

14

# The Animals are Coming Over the Hill

Colour the picture.

15

# Tubby Custard!

Teletubbies love Tubby Custard. But who's slurping it all up? Follow the straws to find out!

# Tinky Winky's Tummy

The Windmill is whirrrrring and someone is appearing on Tinky Winky's tummy. Who do you think it might be?

Stick your favourite picture of yourself on Tinky Winky's tummy.

# Who Spilled The Tubby Custard?

E-oh!

1. One day in Teletubbyland...

2. Tinky Winky saw that somebody had spilled Tubby Custard on the floor.

Uh-oh!

3. But whoever it was, had left footprints.

18

4. Who spilled the Tubby Custard? Tinky Winky followed the footprints.

5. Tinky Winky followed the footprints over the hills.

19

6. Tinky Winky followed the footprints over the hills and around the bush.

7. To the place where Dipsy was sitting with the rabbits.

**8. Was it Dipsy who spilled the Tubby Custard?**

**9. And sure enough, the footprints carried on. Who spilled the Tubby Custard?**

10. The footprints went along the path.

11. Tinky Winky and Dipsy followed the footprints along the path to the place where Laa-Laa was dancing.

12. Was it Laa-Laa who spilled the Tubby Custard?

13. And sure enough, the footprints carried on. Who spilled the Tubby Custard?

14. The footprints went in and out of the trees. Tinky Winky, Dipsy and Laa-Laa followed the footprints in and out of the trees.

15. The footprints went across the path. Tinky Winky, Dipsy and Laa-Laa followed the footprints across the path.

16. The footprints went around the house. Tinky Winky, Dipsy and Laa-Laa followed the footprints around the house.

Uh-oh!

Po!

17. And then they went indoors to the place where Po was fast asleep.

18. Was it Po who spilled the Tubby Custard?

19. Shshshsh! don't wake her.

20. Teletubbies love Po very much. Teletubbies love each other very much.

21. And after all that following footprints around and about, the Teletubbies thought going to sleep was a very good idea indeed.

# Painting with Hands and Feet

These children are painting with their hands and feet.

It looks really messy!

But good fun as well.

Which is your favourite colour?

27

# Finger Painting Fun

Can you paint with your fingers?

Let some paint soak into an old sponge. Press your finger onto the sponge and then onto some paper.

See what happens.

Use different colours on each finger.

Can you fill the page with your finger prints?

Whose are these?

Can you make some?

paint

sponge

saucers for the paint

Can you make a hand print?

Make a big, messy picture!

hedgehog

man in a
funny hat

When the bath is empty,
ask Mummy to tape a
sheet of paper to the tiles.
Then you can make your
hand prints.

Have fun!

# Kites

Read the story in words and pictures.

One day in Teletubbyland, the Teletubbies were flying their kites. The wind blew and 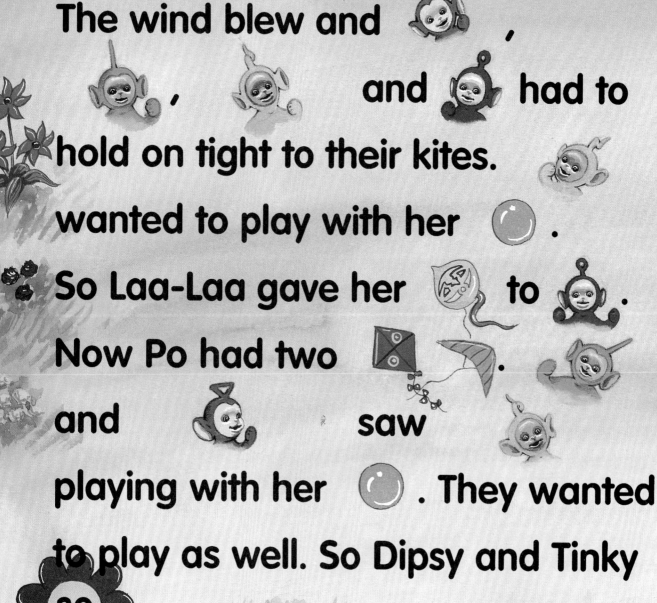 , , and had to hold on tight to their kites.

wanted to play with her .

So Laa-Laa gave her to .

Now Po had two .

and saw

playing with her . They wanted to play as well. So Dipsy and Tinky

30

Winky gave Po their kites too. Now Po was holding all four 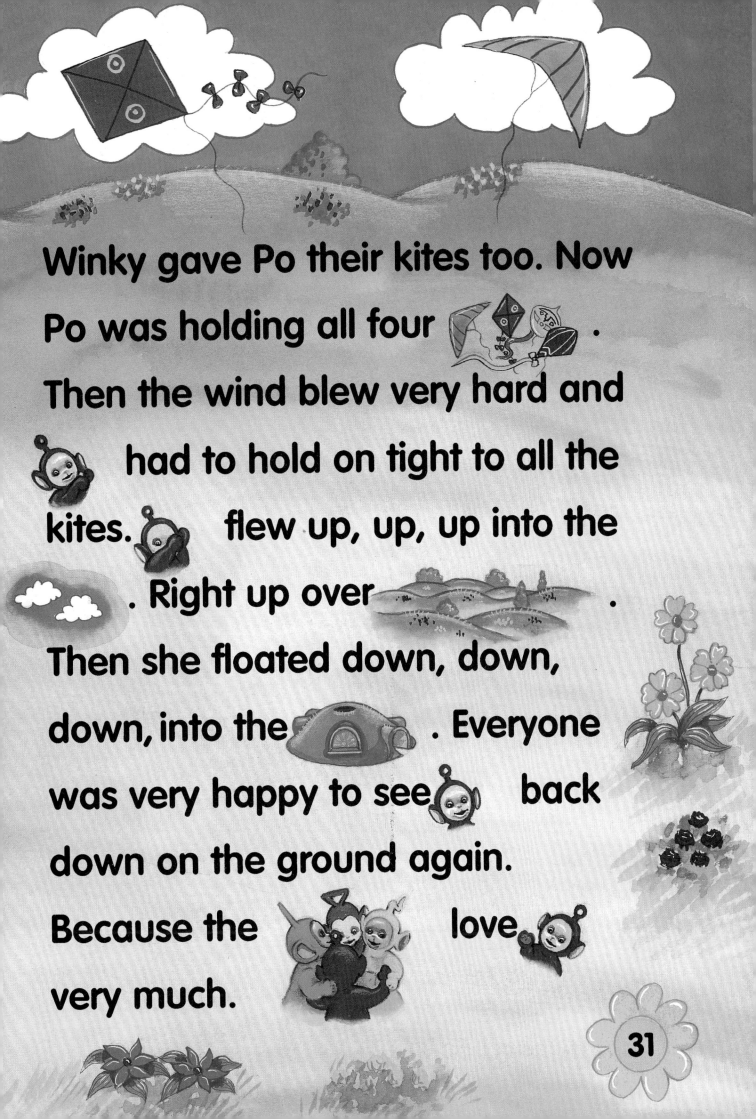 . Then the wind blew very hard and 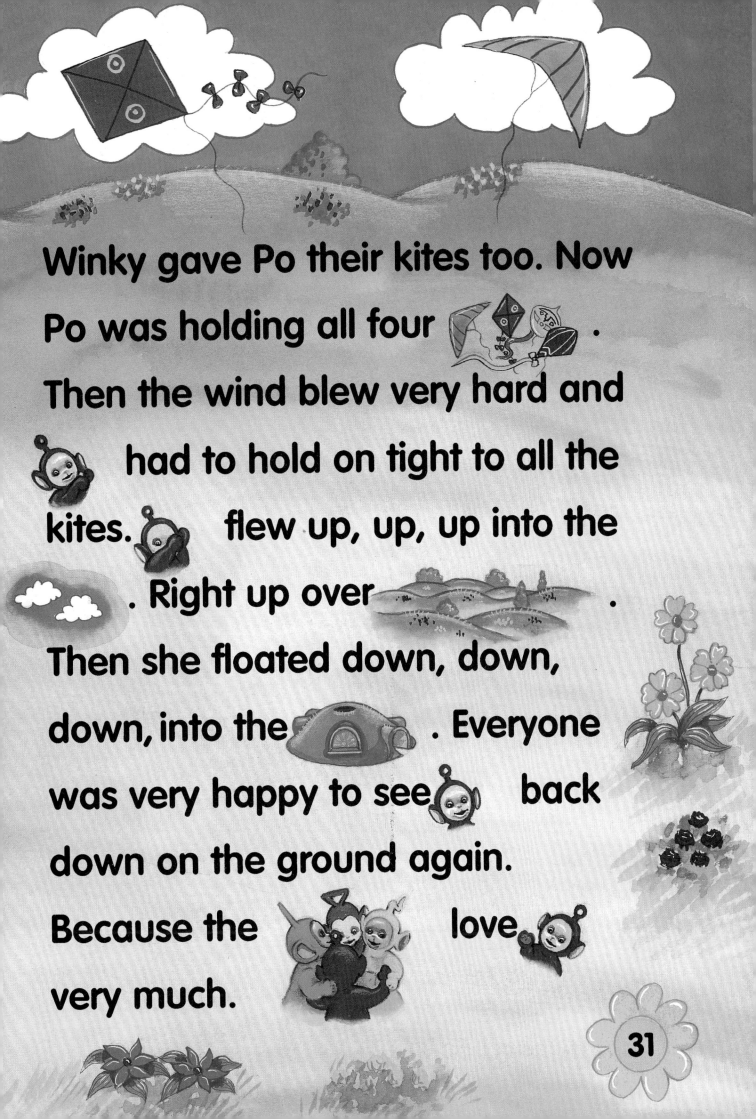 had to hold on tight to all the kites. 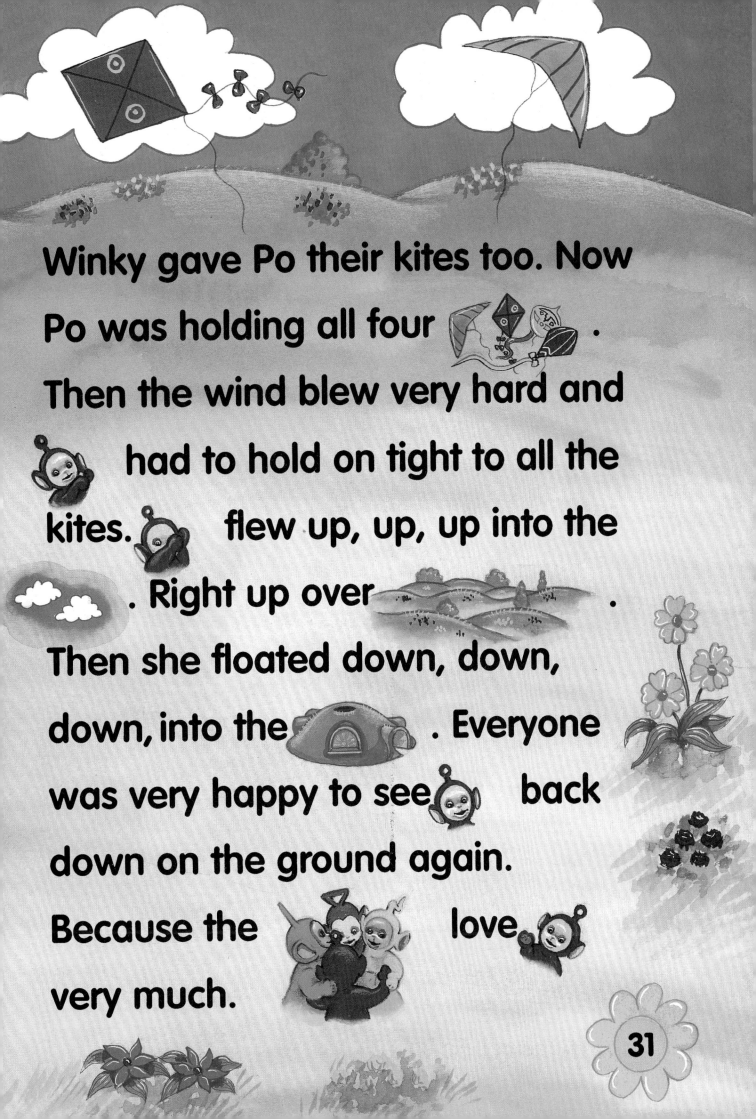 flew up, up, up into the 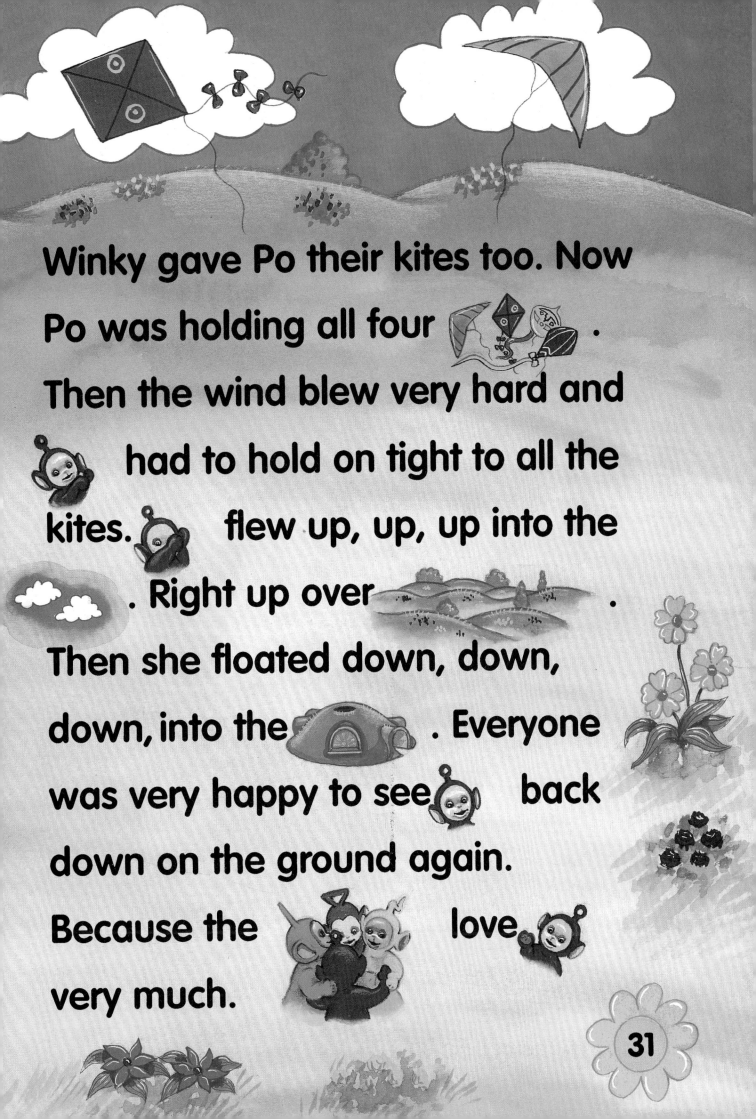 . Right up over 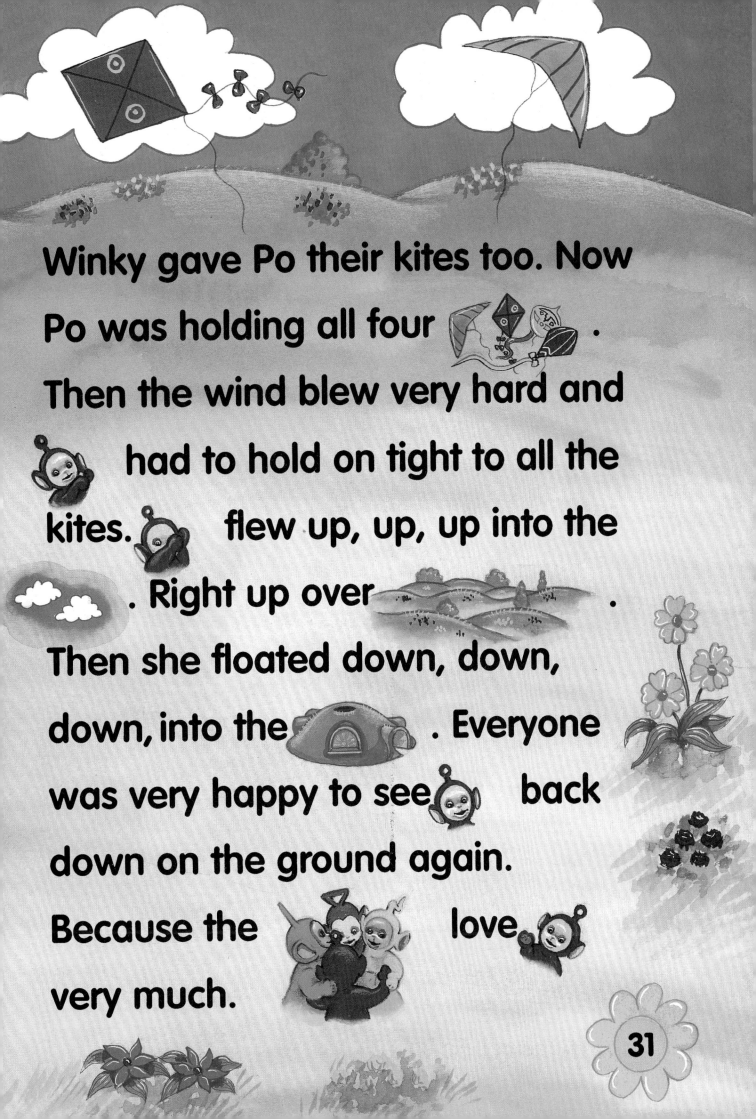 . Then she floated down, down, down, into the 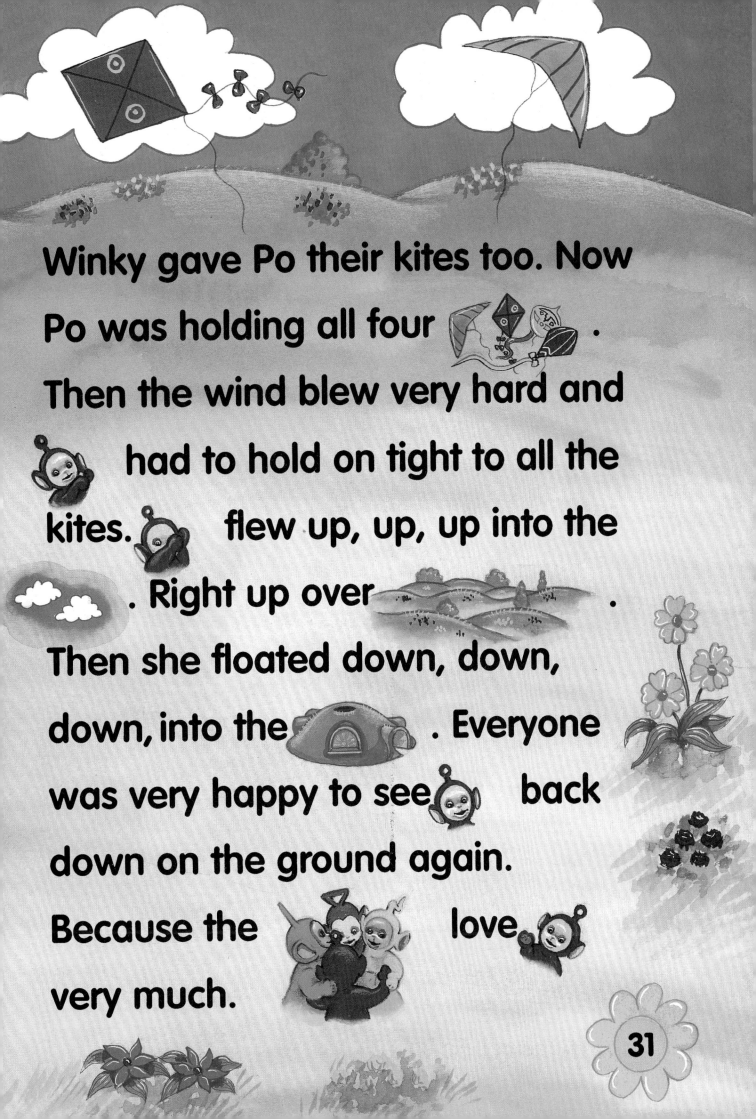 . Everyone was very happy to see 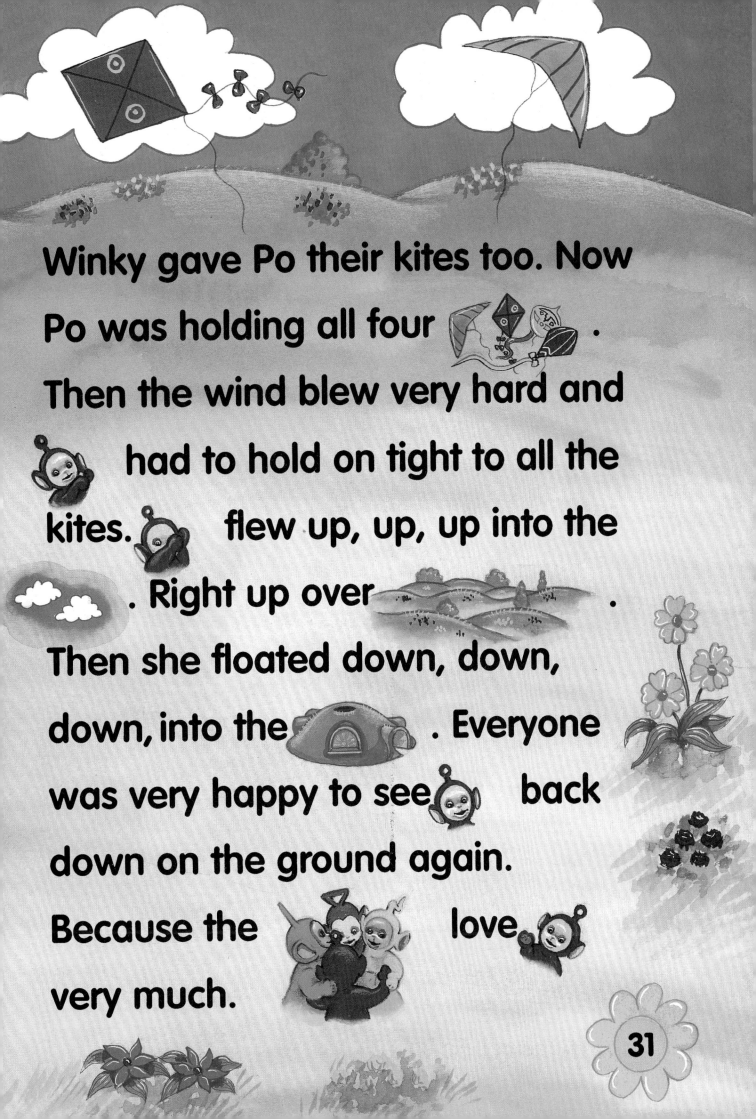 back down on the ground again. Because the 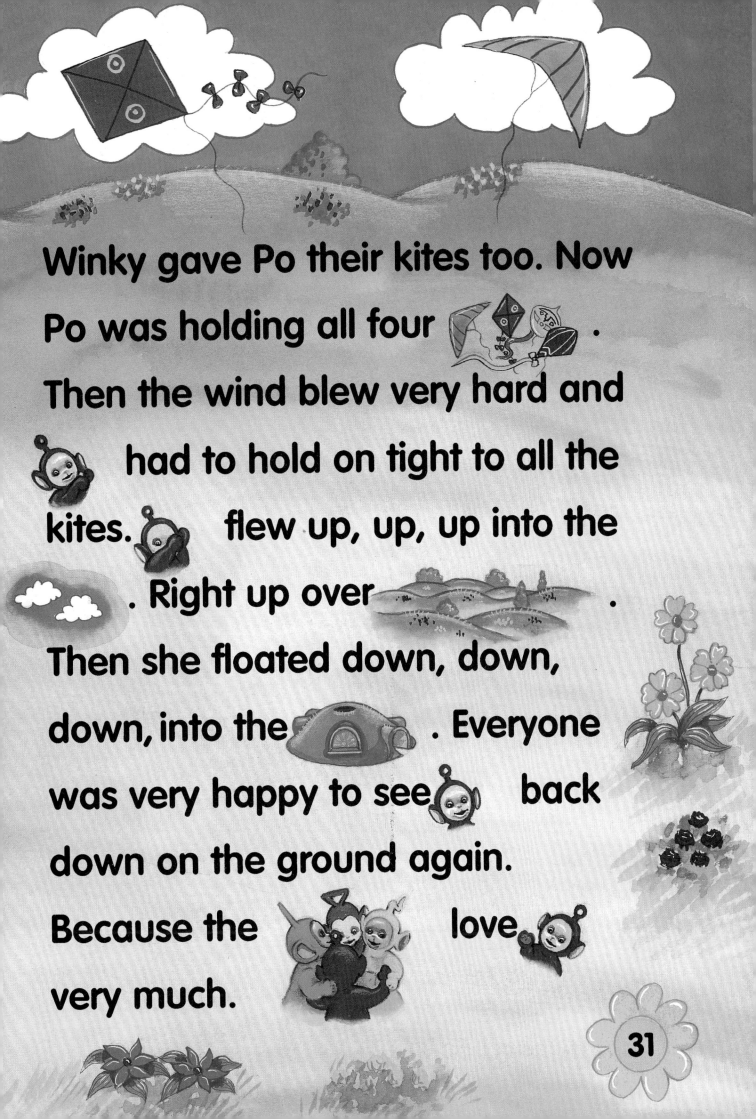 love 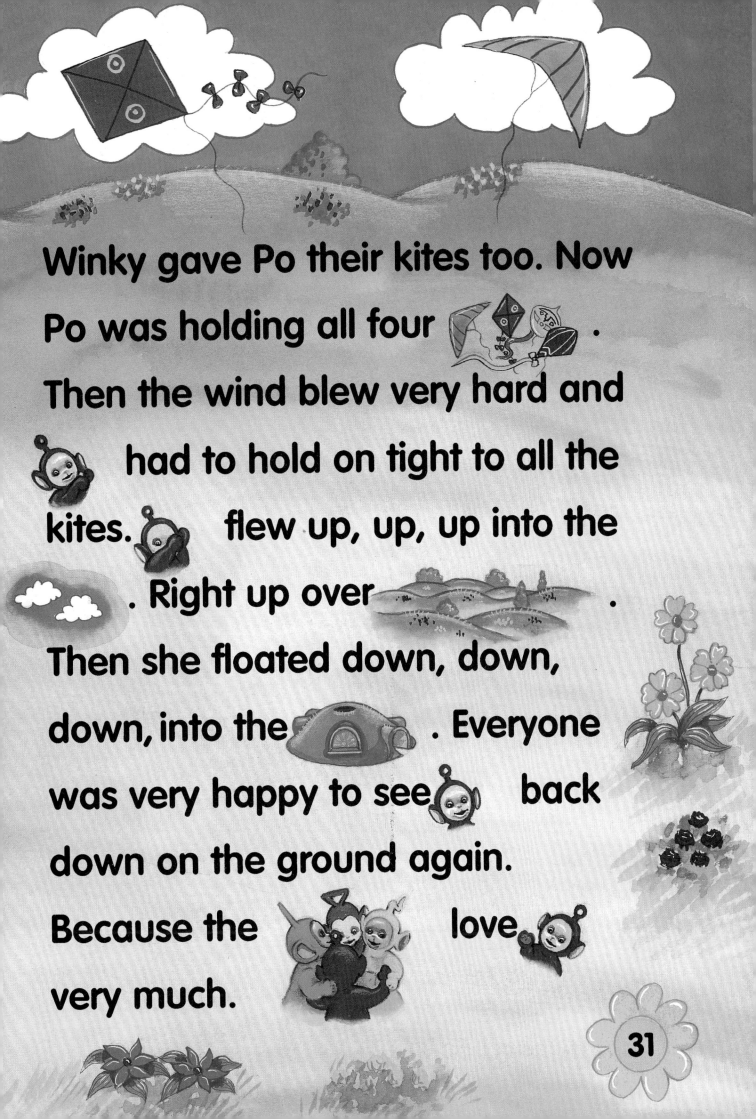 very much.

# Tubby Tangle

How many kites can you count? .............................
Who is holding the purple kite? .............................
Who is holding the green kite? .............................
Who is holding the yellow kite? .............................
Who is holding the red kite? .............................
Who is flying the highest kite? .............................
Who is flying the lowest kite? .............................

# Favourite Things

Teletubbies love their favourite things. Can you match each Teletubby to their favourite thing? One has already been done for you.

What's your favourite thing? Draw a picture of your favourite thing.

# Tubby Toast!

The Teletubbies toaster makes Tubby Toast!
Teletubbies love Tubby Toast!

There are lots of pieces of toast in this picture.
Can you count them?

Twang!

I counted_____ pieces of Tubby Toast.

# Laa-Laa Is Dancing

Draw a line to show where Laa-Laa has been dancing.

Colour in the shapes you make.

LaLaLaLa

35

# Our Favourite Things

**36**

**Laa-Laa**

Po

# Laa-Laa's Watering Can

**1.** One day in Teletubbyland, something new appeared.

**2.** It was a watering can.

3. Laa-Laa watered the yellow flowers.

4. Laa-Laa watered the blue flowers.

Water flowers!

5. There are flowers all over Teletubbyland!

6. Laa-Laa watered lots of flowers until there was no more water left in the watering can.

7. Just then...

Mary Mary quite contrary,
How does your garden grow,
With silver bells,
And cockle shells,
And pretty maids all in a row.

Big Hug!

Laa-Laa loves watering very much! Teletubbies love each other very much.

# Making Flowers

There are flowers all over Teletubbyland.
Make some flowers of your own.

1. Cut out a flower shape
from card using round
ended scissors.

2. Colour your flower.

3. Decorate your flower
with coloured paper,
stickers or sweet wrappers.

4. Use a an ice lolly stick or a straw to make a stem for your flower. Tape your flower on to the stem.

5. You can add leaves or buds if you like.

6. Stick your flower into a blob of dough or modelling clay and put it in a sunny place, so the sun will shine on your flower.

45

# More Flowers!

## Tissue Paper Flowers

You will need:
coloured tissue paper,
tape,
straws or lolly sticks,
round ended scissors

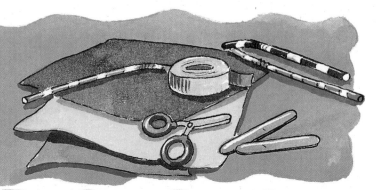

1. Cut out lots of tissue paper flower shapes in different colours and sizes.

4. Keep going until you have a bunch.

2. Put them on top of each other. Twist the centre.

## Torn Paper Flowers

You will need:
coloured paper
gum

3. Tape your flower to a straw or an ice lolly stick.

46

1. Tear some circles and petal shapes out of coloured paper. (It's not as easy as it sounds!)

2. Stick your shapes on to paper and make a flower picture.

## Swirly Flowers

You will need:
coloured paper
a candle or a wax crayon
paint
brush

1. Make some swirly petal shapes with a candle or a wax crayon.

2. Paint over your shapes like this:

## Even More Flowers!

3. Try using a cheese triangles box to make a flower. Decorate it by gluing on pasta shells or rice.

Make lots of flowers!

47

# Don't Step on the

Help Tinky Winky find his way back to the house, without stepping on the flowers.

How many rabbits does he see on the way?

Who can you say hello to?

Be careful!

Bip!

Bip!

Don't tread on us please!

Eek eek eek

48

# Flowers Tinky Winky!

# The Lion and The Bear

I'm the bear with fuzzy brown hair, I'll hide over here and I'll hide over there.

The bear is hiding from the lion, can you see her?

I am the scary lion with big scary teeth, I'm scary on the top and I'm scary underneath!

Who else can you see?

51

Teletubbies™

**Noo-noo**

52

# Naughty Noo-noo

1. One Day in Teletubbyland, the Tubbies heard somebody coming.

2. It was the Noo-noo.

Slurp Slurp

3. The Noo-noo was tidying up.

54

6. Naughty Noo-noo.

Sluuuuurrrp

bagat bagat gah gah hag

7. When the Noo-noo had tidied up the bag and the hat, he tidied up the ball.

Sluuurrrp

56

8. "Naughty Noo-noo," said the Teletubbies.

Naughty Noo-noo

9. Naughty, naughty Noo-noo.

laggab laggab tah tah gah

57

Slurp Slurp laggab laggab tah tah gab

10. And the Teletubbies chased the Noo-noo round and round the house.

11. Round and round and round the house, until he gave back all their things.

Slurp Slurp Slurp laggab laggab slurp Slurp

What's that noise?

**12. Teletubbies love Noo-noo very much.**

Big hug

Slurp Slurp Slurp Slurp

**13. And Teletubbies love each other very much.
Use your pens or crayons and colour in the Tubbies.**

fffff   Big hug   fffff

Lovely

Slurp Slurp

59

# Tubby Bye-Bye

**Bye-Bye Laa-Laa!**

Bye-Bye

Time for Tubby
Bye-Bye
Time for Tubby
Bye-Bye
Time for Tubby
Bye-Bye

# Goodnight Game

Help put the Tubbies to bed by playing their goodnight game. You need a spinner or a dice and some buttons. Decide who is going to be Tinky Winky, Dipsy, Laa-Laa or Po and place the buttons on the starting space. Throw the dice once each, the highest number starts. After that, take turns. The first to reach their bed is the winner!
If you land on a piece of Tubby Toast, shout 'Tubby Toast! Tubby Toast!' and move forward three spaces. If you land on a space with a flower on it, miss one turn to look at the flowers.

Po's Scooter! Whizz forward 4 spaces

8

7

6

5

3

start

11

13

15

bip! bip